Self-Portrait with Severed Head

First Printing January, 2009
ISBN 978-0-578-00198-2
Library of Congress Control Number: 2008943910

Published by
Ibbetson Street Press
25 School Street
Somerville, MA 02143
617.628.2313

Self-Portrait with Severed Head

Poems
by
C. D. Collins

Ibbetson Street Press · Somerville, Massachusetts

Also by C. D. Collins

Slow Burn *(1997)*
Kentucky Stories *(1999)*
Subtracting Down *(2004)*
Carousel Lounge *(2008)*
Blue Land *(2009)*

Acknowledgments

Grateful acknowledgment is made to the editors of the following publications in which some of these poems have appeared: *Blue Unicorn; Poetry, People & the Plagues, MCET Anthology; Spoken Live!* compilation disc with the Jeff Robinson Trio; *The Boston Poet; The Boston Poet Journal: Virgin Voyage; the Cambridge Tab; "Lyric Somerville," Somerville News; Ibbetson Street;* and *Provincetown Magazine.*

"The Fox" was awarded Best Love Poem at the Cambridge Poetry Awards 2003.

"Blood Orange" musical version featured on NPR's *Here and Now.*

Thanks to the Writers' Room of Boston, Wellspring House, and Duxbury Writers' Colony, where many of these poems were written.

Profound gratitude to Pamela Painter, Lexa Marshall, Jenny Barber, Linda Cutting, and Carol Dine for their support of my work.

Special thanks to the musicians who have collaborated with me to transform the written word into spoken songs: Chris Burleson; Patrice Williamson; members of Pincurl: Sandy Zaragoza, Audrey Tang, Ellen Klein, Carol DeFeciani, and Carolyn Castellano; members of Rockabetty: John Minkle, Yani Batteau, Noor O'Neill Borbeiva, Zack Niman, Teddy Ansbacher-Hunt, John Wilde, and my brothers in poetry jam, the inimitable Jeff Robinson Trio.

Photographs

Babette Meyers
"Self-Portrait with Severed Head" *(Front cover)*
"Amelia" *(Element)*
"Gina" *(Incognito)*
"Laura" *(Prodigal)*

Jaime Malzman
"C. D. at Berklee" *(Spoken Songs)*

James Blandini & Libbie Sherman
"C. D. in Red Coat" *(Back cover)*

Book Design

Cover
Libbie Sherman & Allison Lund

Editing, layout
Danny Marcus

Graphics
Steve Glines

for Eight Belles and the innocents*

"She ran with the heart of a locomotive,
on champagne-glass ankles."

Sally Jenkins,
Washington Post

* Eight Belles, February 23, 2005 – May 3, 2008. Thoroughbred Eight Belles collapsed suddenly after finishing second in the 134th running of the Kentucky Derby. The three-year old filly suffered compound fractures in both front ankles and was euthanized on the track.

Contents

Element

Mime

By the way she moves in air,
a mime may create stairs, a lover, a city.
So I will fashion a self
to solace and protect;
I will create from nothing ever learned,

But wholly needed.

I begin with a nod,
a Phoebe of imagined warmth.

My Mother's Dogs

Don't you hear them?
Did you think I wouldn't?
Their parched tongues worry my sleep.

My hands chafed in wind
as I pushed brass anchor buttons
through buttonholes like nooses
draped over soldered cellar pipes.
I cut the ropes each time and held you close,
as though I were someone who could stay with you,
hoping you wouldn't notice I'd spilled hot chocolate
down my wool plaid skirt, brand new.

It didn't matter that your dogs
pushed their wet noses up taboo crevices
decapitated your prized flowers
with one whip of their spiky tails.

I snatched my diary from
Ollie Russell's nail-bitten hands.
He'd read it out loud, already, to the boys,
who threw pennies at little Robby Martin
crouching by the wall with his harmonica
his notes melting into silver flux.

I retrieved my book locked with a counterfeit key,
but only to bury it in my drawer.
What made me think I'd be protected?
You'd read it too,
then told me I couldn't play
with the Toomey twins again.

I would hide my words then;
I would drown your Dachshunds in the swimming pool.
I see now that you were too distracted

to realize the shock of your flat hand.
You couldn't help yourself,
couldn't help the hitting
couldn't help favoring them.

You hear them, don't you?
crying beneath the rose quartz in the garden
under full-blown, shaggy, iris blooms.

Your dogs could not resist you,
ate through wire mesh at the veterinarian
while you were on vacation;
ate through leather interiors
of Lincoln Continentals
while you were in the drug store;
ate through apartment doors
until the neighbors had you evicted.

When you came home they trailed behind you;
nails ticked down the marble hallway,
poised on their haunches for trimmed fat scraps,
scorched morsels you'd taught me to covet, too.

Their chests heaved and trembled,
measuring the frenzy of *your* hunger.
They were the ones who never had to forgive.
Don't you hear them?
I do.

Subtracting Down

I love the way I can
drag a screw
through soap
tap a starter nail in the wall
drive the screw into the stud,
the way the men talk about studs
when they build houses,

pouring the footer
framing up the 2x4s
laying in studs.

He asks his wife,
You getting stud service
from Tommy Banta,
who wears
the red stone,
a bleeding garnet
in his solid gold ring.

Tommy Banta,
who drives her to work
pulls into
the KFC drive-through
whispers into the speaker
I'll have a breast, he says,
and fries.

I love the way peace floats
settling on the furniture
the velvet armchair
subtracting down.

Don't dick around with the figures, baby;
you don't know how it's going to all add up.

He says, Y*ou know, if it weren't for me,*
there'd be no high rise;
all be living under a dome of sky.
I say,
I love when my own fear speaks, says,
hiding *will not protect you.*
We find our way
through subtraction
stripping down.

I love the fragrance of grease
from exhaust fans
into the winter morning,
walking past on my way to the factory,
how steam billows into clouds
my hands
two blue stars
in my coat pockets.

In my bones I carry
the habits
of my precious desolation.

Time dissolves
undifferentiated
water on water
white on white.

I will drain the disturbances
like polluted oil,
eroding the pistons
the corroded washers
the sick engine.

I will loosen the bolt
drain the accumulation
the bitter screws.

In the blighted bayou
a man floats
in the orange fungus,
rocking face up
in the dinghy's wake.

Do you love the way
we find
our way
through
subtraction?

The men full of friction
building the world
the screws
the studs
the 2x4s.

I love the
erosion
the attrition
the rusting
the stripping down,

till there is nothing
left but essence.
Nothing to save,
nothing to hide,
nothing to fear.

Diamonds

are so necessary,
for cutting emeralds, rubies, glass,
the perfect substance for the task.
Give me diamond chips in a velvet box,
I'll grind them with my eyes to dust.

I remember when the tone arm clicked,
the 45 ejector slipped
the record down its sliding pole
to spin on dusty Rubber Soul.
A diamond meant the truest sound
for vinyl spinning round and round,
Come on, baby, let's do the Twist,
James Dean look-alike, who could resist?
A smile so bright,
his smooth, broad brow
he lay me down;
he show me how.

"Don't you feel it?" he always asked,
his skin so bronze, those dark eyelashes,
"Yes," was not quite what I meant
as he unzipped my pants with the circus tents.

Friday evenings to the downtown dance,
his sapphire eyes, his tight-legged pants,
the back door slammed, but in mid-air
a scent like gunpowder from his hair.
At recess, dancing in a gang
to songs that Chubby Checker sang
confessed what I dared not reveal
through rhythms that my limbs could feel.
Good-looking boys just turned nineteen
cannot escort someone so green

too young for hips or even breasts
who wore pants sewn with circus tents.
I learned my lessons well back then,
to do lots of things without feeling them,
and how to shut my senses down
so well no one can hurt me now.
Give me promises, jeweled rings.
Touch me. I don't feel a thing.

Diamonds aren't so necessary now,
hard gems are carved by light somehow,
songs spun by lasers, from dust withdrawn
like secrets, too bright to look upon.
Diamonds cut stones softer than they,
scratch dust from grooves, make old songs play,
dug from deep in veins like he mined me,
but diamonds aren't as necessary as they used to be.

At ten, I waited for my debut,
on the dance floor at Teen Rendezvous.
The ball of mirrors, swirling light,
still beckons me on Friday nights.
He'll cross the floor in his Sixties best,
his open shirt, his chestnut chest,
"Don't you feel it?" he'll ask again,
his sweat like sugar on my skin,
his hands so sure, his eyes dusk blue,
I couldn't feel it, but I wanted to.

The Twist in its groove, an unfinished song,
that James Dean face, forever young,
what would I say had I the chance,
to speak to him over thirty years past,
as the woman I am, no longer ten,
who learns to feel in spite of him.
I'll extend my hand, give him the chance,
to see how well that kid could dance.

I'll close the years we've been apart,
I'll lay his hand against my heart
"Don't you feel it?" I'll ask once more,
of that teenager now turned fifty-four,

whose image is constant in memory,
"How many days in a thousand do you think of me?"
"How many days, I just wanted to know."
Then I'll finish the song, and I'll let him go.

Dreaming in My Mother's House

Early,
the pine trees mark black against
blue light outside the glass doors
half moon and mist,
almost six o'clock.
I see her
blue robe, blue smoke,
blue, first color that emerges from the gray.

I slide a cigarette from her pack
flick her brass lighter,
draw on the spicy, edifying smoke.

"You should give up cigarettes," I say to her.

"I quit for six months," she answers,
sliding the door open to let in her cat.
"Drinking, too. Then I realized I might live longer."

I'd been dreaming
that vultures roosted
in all the trees in Philadelphia;
magnificent vultures,
with downy feathers like fur,
eagle's heads,
but vultures still.
So big, four of them could spread
wings wide enough to gather
the tallest building in the city,
an apocalypse of beautiful vultures.

From the highway,
we could see another plane go down
behind a row of suburban houses.

People pulled their cars onto the shoulder,
mesmerized by the enormous birds.

Someone was driving, some important lover.
Driving, napping, driving.
"Wake up," I shouted, shaking his shoulders.
"Wake up and look."
"Mother,
do you remember the time you fell on glass,
the red blood on the walk,
red dress, red lips,
kaleidoscopic jewel pinned to your breast?"
Blood ran from the walk into the dirt,
scoring a line between us.

Now grandmother bangs on the floor,
with her cane in the other room.
She lists the highways back to California;
she is driving there tomorrow.
She's always on her way somewhere.
She's going to dig for mussels at Prince Edward Island,
To Maine, her studio by the lake,
Always going home.

I touch my mother's robe,
old chenille, pull her tight.
I am taller than she is now.
But she is stronger,
From mowing the orchard, shoveling sod,
From digging roots with bare hands.

In my other dream,
I'm in Kentucky,
sitting outside the Episcopal church,
Early light, the same as now,
blue with black trees and the moon.

I wear elaborate rings on my hand,
carved ivory and jade.
Old friends surround me.
"It's the tintinnabulum of rings," I say.
The children sing in unison,
and out of the church come the beautiful horses
with red plumes and golden bridles with jewels dangling,
and they climb with their elegant hooves into the sky.

Sunday Noon

During his long months of dying,
my father showered and shaved
every morning by nine,
dressed in his best clothes
he'd laundered and pressed,
drove his battered truck around town
the day before his last.

How like him,
this cat too weak to walk
still grooming in her litter box.

Their wiry will and pulse
savored daily routine as
the best pleasure
of this ebbing world.

I missed my father's death
by fifteen minutes
last Easter noon,
I should have known.

His children had both been born
at Sunday noon,
which meant, he said,
we could see leprechauns.

Every cat is a Southern lady,
knows how to pick the spot in each room
to best exhibit her beauty.
Brown paw against white leather;
blue eyes overlooking the sea.

I learned to pluck a tent of shoulder skin,
punch in the needle drip,

dilute poisoned blood,
pills to flush
her overworked heart.
After the funeral
deep in my father's wallet
pictures of my brother and me
from Junior High.
Until I held them,
I had not imagined
he'd ever thought of us.

Returning to Boston,
midnight in the hotel,
the thump of a fall
from the tub's edge wakes me.
I pick her up
lay her gently on the carpet
in a narrow slice of moon.

I trace my lips along her fur.
My chocolate-brownie ears,
my groundhog, my possum,
my heart.

This last touch like a lover's
trembling and exotic
as the first.

Kneeling blindly in the dark,
I am the one who stays,
still hostage to this world.

Spoken Songs

Self-Portrait with Severed Head

Sometimes when hunters fail at the trigger,
and lose their blood heat,
they shoot with a camera instead.

To touch is to change.

My hands waver in the shrill metals,
swirl the poisons till the image floats up to me.

I imagine all our cascading faces,
smiling larger than ourselves,
fixed and absorbed through my eye,
and think how small
our souls must be by now.

Eclipse

Tonight a shadow covers the moon;
the shadow, just a shadow, the world.
The moon is full and singing its familiar song of O's.
The voice vibrates in the hard cavities
until the planet seems to live.
There is a woman walking under the moon
in the barren streets of the town
as the shadow bites into the bright edges.

You could say:
this woman traverses the sky
long trails of light years
weaving themselves into her hammock.
You could say
her heart was the moon
cold and bright,
or her eye in one-quarter view.
Yet these are only images.

The light of the moon is a dust of glass
reflecting a distant star;
the moon's surface slippery, like silica,
faintly reflective, like volcanic sand.
You could say the moon always shows the same face,
as it revolves with the earth
in the light of the home star.
You could say,
yet this is only science.

The shadow muffles the light like a hand of smoke
until the voice is small, a reverberation.
She steps into a doorway out of the wind
listens as the voices rise from the craters—
Sea of Clouds, Sea of Showers, Ocean of Storms.

She hears the song about hushed deaths
and persistent shadows;
the song about the seed that must grow
to the size of a galaxy
in one lifetime.
So that it may contain this:
astonishing, temporary, illumination.

The Back of His Mind

Through his head
I could see the shapes
passing trees,
phone poles.
The wires strung rhythmically to their moorings.
Mounting, descending,
knots catching, not missing a beat,
high wires, hands joining,
like a human chain.

Through the gray head,
shaggy, clay-like,
with the flap lifted,
I could observe another dusk,
attend the cadence
the pum, pum, pum,
while the horizon rolled her hot gold
into a nest
and sank beyond the trees
moss
swamp.

The music with cellos,
slow drums and sticks on metal,
wondering
if it glowed beneath, a hot god.
With the flap of his head
up like that

I could see in to the back of his mind,
that the west balled into yellow
and was sinking,
that the clouds were igniting
an icy gold, with pink fire curling,
while I listened to the drums,
and darkening,
while I watched them burning.

Everyeye

This is the eye that is part of the wood,
a knot of the wood;
I feel it during the night when the paint chips,
I smooth it down; it is my eye.

I am walking through a tunnel;
it is my prison. I feel it with my fingers.
I am walking down a highway.
I am walking down a hallway.
I am walking down a path in the sand,
a path made by horses.
Horses are hard on the land.
I can see but my eyes are closed.
I can see but I keep my eyes in my pocket.

On my bedstand, an oval-shaped grain in the wood,
a knot where a limb once grew,
this is my eye.
It is painted over and I keep it there, hidden,
it knows everything I know and cannot know,
everything I do not wish to know.

I have painted over it and the paint is smooth,
I feel it in the dark when I cannot see.
Trust can be fractured like opals,
the moist flames leak out;
the paint peels, it is my eye trying to look.

The shivering membranes will loosen
but forcing ruins the soft tissues of opening and closing,
then it can never rest, never be blind,
the eye that is meant to open and to close,
to see, not to see,
and to choose.

Slow Burn

Inside the stone wall / behind the gray door /
the skillful doctor / who is a fancier /
of our fine tattoos / removes and cures:
a flying eagle / a heart with arrows / a crimson rose.

Behind the iron gate / they're testing shoe soles /
on broken limestone / on cinders, cobblestones /
they wear forty-pound weights / so they can compensate /
for all that lost weight / they walk ten hours a day /
we want them all to see / that work shall make them free.

Behind the block wall / inside the sealed room /
they have to hurry now / they have to pile us up /
they have to slide us in / like racks of gingerbread /
we burn so slowly.

We give you everything / we give our thick hair /
we give our smooth skin / we light the walkways /
of well-fed night guards / with steel-tipped bullets /
who feed in hard logs / we burn so slowly.

We've had to squander them / we're in a hurry /
we've had to file them in / we've had to pile them up /
we've had to slide them in / like racks of gingerbread /
they burn so slowly.

We give them everything / our steel-tipped bullets /
we give the hard logs / inside the stone wall /
behind the iron gate / within the block wall /
behind the gray door / inside the sealed room /
we have to hurry now / we have to stack them up /
we have to slide them in / they burn so slowly.

Now we all file down / into the station /
a list of towns here / but no one looks now /

the trains don't stop there / we comb our thick hair /
we oil our smooth skin / our bodies 98 / degrees of slow burn /
we have forgotten / we're in a hurry /
we give up everything / we burn so slowly.

Demimonde

Tornado pulse points
giant finger
directing school bus
girl with satchel
plaid skirt

while inside
Dominican mother
sips espresso
from rich glazed
demitasse.
Underground seeking missiles
wishing her daughter
skates.

Silver blades
land with spray and flourish
as though rising
were effortless
inevitable
possible.

I came to your country,
loved the smell
of curing meat,
boiled sugar cane,
jasmine in the rain,
spiced rum and swollen fruit.

Loved the look
of houses exploded
by tropical storms
built back in various pastel
pink shingle
pale blue post

from Manolito's
chicken coop.
One pound per day
I shed
in Puerto Plata
Santo Domingo
dining on *platanos*
Coca-Cola.

We're helping them,
our hosts claimed
of the ten-year-old
servant girls
in the house with
laces of wrought iron gates,
rows of locks
too hot to touch.

Christmas morning
our car broke mid-island.
They'll think you're the
Virgin Mary
in your white gown
on the mountain.
Pink-skinned,
your hair stains the air
like saffron.

They'll arrive
on motorcycles
burros,
drive pickups
with children
who will die
of colds
and hookworm,
women bound

for America,
demimondes
of demiworlds
with the divining rods
of their spread legs,
who will tell themselves
that doing this is a way
of stopping doing this.

You will hear
the demisemiquaver
life-span
a thirty-second note
when they
reach hands
inside the car,
pull your blond hair
for luck, *Claro,*
you're not real,
you are a vision.

The Blues

If Mama Cass had given Karen Carpenter that ham sandwich,
*They'd both be alive today.**

Don't you remember those parties
in the Seventies where the beauty ideal
was like an IV drug user with skinny hips,
tight pants with giant bell-bottoms that surely tolled for You.
You were there, or your older sister,
baby brother, or your son, the one assigned a 4-F
for acting crazy like he didn't want to
sacrifice his body for a face like LBJ's.

But you do remember in the back seat when his live
cigarette ash accidentally dropped on your nylons,
the lines of fire zipping up your legs,

You remember how you smiled,
because you knew already;
no one had to say it.

So you were there
in the back seat
comparing thighs.
Yours were wider.

You needed to be smaller than him
so he could protect you.
Once he starved himself for a month,
eating only bananas.
He was a pacifist.
He looked like Jesus,
with his long hair and suffering face.

You listened to Abbey Road and Purple Haze,
hands dancing in the light of the strobe candle.

You wore his jeans now and they were loose on you.
You laughed at Karen Carpenter,
and Mama Cass was warning boys with her big mouth,
and Janis said what Karen couldn't.
You listened to their voices,
described them like wine.
At least they had voices,
you seemed to lose yours,
drinking White Russians in snowstorms, running fast,
tripping over something you didn't see
and falling like Dick Van Dyke,
except you hit hard
and Mary Tyler Moore was not in the kitchen.
It was you preparing dinners,
but you didn't eat them.

Then it wasn't just rainy days and Mondays that got you down,
it was sunny days and Saturday nights,
that seemed to accuse.
You filled the room
with the white spew of what you'd always been fed,
then lay down on your chaste bed
half-sleeping, listening to the radio.
In the candlelight an aqua aura encircled your head,
like the Saturn's rings.
What I got
They used to call the blues.
You had to admit you liked that voice,
it had a finish of something you craved.
It was like being hungry in church when you were ten,
so you invented foods,
for every word the preacher chanted—
sweet rhubarb Ruth
King Solomon cole slaw
good dark bread in the House of David,
River Jordan almond

land of milk and honey.
It was Karen, singing,
in the end she looked like your old boyfriend, Jesus.
You are starving,
she is singing,
and this is what you ate.

**joke in the public domain*

Blood Orange

Beyond the jobs,
the traffic, the wind,
beyond aqua stars
I'll let you spin
like a cosmonaut into ether,
released without a sound.

When I finish you,
no longer this anchor of memory.
When I finish you,
glass covenants crushed into comets by my hands.

My hands will forget
what I held right here,
how I never looked
but I knew you were there,
how the moon dipped low,
dissolved in dark wine.

When I finish you,
when the sun splits into blood oranges.
When I finish you,
when we have suckled its seismic velvet.

When I can't loosen,
when I can't give,
storms will descend
flaring the banks of the river
non-coterminous blue

When I finish you,
asking nothing of you.
When I finish you,
at last loving you.

Beyond the jobs,
the traffic, the wind,
beyond aqua stars
I'll let you spin
like falling
like falling.

Spanish Mountain

Terraces are steps
oleander is spun sugar
walking stick is metronome
pomegranate is promise
clementines are children
arroyo are tender spokes
hibiscus is offered kiss

Fig leaf is palm
olive trunks are gray scars
date palm is silver
avocado is mirror
root is philosopher

Crest is silence
Mediterranean is horseshoe
houses are sweet chalk

Roof tiles are candy sticks
sun is white smoke
God is broom dust
marble chip is dawn shard
sleep is colossus

Incognito

City of Dreams

I wait
in the gloaming
of the fairy's lantern.
Steal in beside me,
cup my body
with your body of light.
For you,
I open the passage to my city of dreams.
What is the spark that lights this place?
It is the quick, the filament
that burns through the cage of night,
illuminates the path
where you discover me
where I discover you.

Incognito

I enter the house
climb the stairs
the common space of a city
tells a story,
urban fluids and crystal urine,
the smell of smoke,
places no one feels responsible for.

I knock on the unpainted door.
She opens,
blue eyes, mascara,
full lips, but something tortured.

In my dream
our eyes meet, we touch hands
we cannot stop touching.

I climb the stairs.
Is there anybody there?
I am knocking on your door.
She opens the door.

The boy with his dark mane
hands me a sword,
wants me to teach him
how the ancient masters
spring to the tops of buildings
duel on ceramic-tiled roofs
how they humbly bow,
but I am not welcome here.

How did this happen,
that I am the renegade exiled
from a house of renegades?
This happened

because that's the way it works.
Erase the face
until you can't see yourself there.
I enter the stairwell
climb the stairs
I too have lied
because I could not live with consequence.
I too have hidden,
a coward with a closed, chaotic heart.

They boarded the plane,
moved incognito
in shadows and blue shirts.
Did you think you could get safe inside your house?

I believe that evil is more powerful than good,
I heard someone say.
Perhaps evil possesses more force.
Perhaps our good is too, passive, too inert.

We watch, re-watch,
the pale skin of the building,
the shiny skin,
the happy contours
of the steady little plane.
I see buildings
I see water
Oh my God.
That is what we say
to express the inexpressible
Allah, we say,
we are high as the stratosphere,
we are drunk as kings.
Our flame evaporates crystal steel
deeper, higher,
to the place where we all connect.

If I die, will you listen?
If I die, will you understand?

I thought invisibility,
I thought anonymity,
would save my skin,
The skin of the building
the shiny skin,
we see buildings,
we see water,
Oh my God.
This is what we say
to replace the irreplaceable.

I imagine that world does not end,
does not go dark;
that we see ourselves
hauled up,
tumbling with the good ceramic cups,
flight wings that mean all is well.

The boy steps forward,
hands me a silver sword.
We jump to the tops of buildings,
we break through steel with our palms.
Imagine your hand where you want it to go.
Imagine it unharmed on the other side.
How they joined hands and jumped,
leaving the future behind them.

I climb the stairs.
Is there anybody there?
The sky exploding blue.

I enter the building
climb the stairs
the common space of the city tells a story;

diesel dust,
flinty grit hanging in the air,
places that no one feels responsible for.

I smell of wine,
of shards of bone.
I smell of evaporated steel.
You are frightened by my broken strangeness.

"Oh my God," you say.

Who am I but a woman in America
who owns her own body and desire,
who owns work of my hands.

Though broken
I must believe the promise between us,
this fragile bridge
is all we have.
I spread my arms open.
I swallow flame
place my hand on your shoulder
follow you through smoke.
Open the door, welcome me in.
It is the only way to survive beyond the end.

Aquamarine

The first time I heard the Rolling Stones
I was over at the Jacksons' basement
Tina Jackson's eyes so big and black,
they were like complex eyes, like Atom Ant;
but my boyfriend was Timmy Simpson,
my boyfriend was Jimmy Paul Peyton,
my boyfriend was Jesse Ramsey.
Jesse played a drum set, red sparkle,
Jesse replaced the gear-shift knob on his Mustang, red sparkle.

I dated the tall boys, you know why?
'Cause they could rebound the ball
and zing it to me at half-court,
which was made of concrete, 'cause we were outside,
'cause there was no girl's basketball,
so I had to be cheerleader,
to spread-eagle off the round trampoline.
Missy was my brother's girlfriend.
She was alarmed by a lightning bug
she thought was dive-bombing the slumber party and singing
"YOU TELLING LIES" from some pop song,
Oh yeah, the Beatles. "I'm down, I'm really down."

Yeah, my brother was down as he put on his class ring,
the one Missy returned with the angora snipped off
then put his fist through the wall of his bedroom,
the wide end a wall all glass with sliding doors,
so we could see the magnolias and
the swimming pool built by Futura—
almost like a real pool
like the city pool with the high dive.
Jesse beat his sister twelve ways from Wonder Bread
'cause I kept asking her on our dates to the drive-in
we didn't have DVDs then,

didn't try to fast-forward our lives
by laying our thumbs on the remote
trying to get to the good part.
Time was longer then.
Her blue eyes were like water behind glass that is breaking,
black mascara making her face harsh at fifteen.

When Jesse was finished,
she put on her long coat
and walked down the asphalt
pavement of Fairlawn to my house.
She walked past Jimmy Paul Peyton's house
with the speedboat.
He sang, *Come on down to my boat, baby,* like a stupid.
He was from Virginia.
His family spent Christmas in Daytona.
I'd worn his letter sweater.
Past the Jacksons' house with their groovy basement and
groovy mother, where we danced to the Rolling Stones.

I didn't like the Rolling Stones,
didn't like the way the music hammered on my synapses,
reprogramming the grooves in my brain.
Yet some songs'll take hold, and won't leave me alone,
I crave 'em like swimming
and whispers at the drive-in.

If their mother hadn't died that year,
she would have stopped Jesse.
If their father had been home, not on a date,
all skinny with grief.

When Timmy Simpson overhanded the ball
over the heads of the red team,
I could hit them continuously
from the outside, from half-court.
I could come continuously,

but only in fantasy
where Jimmy Paul Peyton unbuttoned my shirt
his breath all smoky
like when he came
into Mrs. Hayes's typing class as the bell rang,
his hair shiny as pulled taffy
and sat right in front of me.
She walked past Sammy Maxwell's house
in her coat with gold buttons,
Sammy, whom she would later marry and have
babies that I would never see.

She knocked on my glass door
and woke me from a dream
where I had brown eyes
and was Catholic;
a dream of being Jewish,
of living with the black folks in Foxville, of belonging.
She slid open the door over which I never drew the curtains
because I wanted to see what was out there
opened the door and let in a wall of dark water
in slow motion, like Jell-O,
then slid into bed beside me,
all bruised, cut, and shaken.
I realized then what happened when people
ran out of places to store longing.
Jesse, lost in his backyard like a villain without his glasses,
understood why I wanted us both to be good girls,
not replace our mothers with schoolboys,
understood why she wouldn't speak to me after that,
not ever and not now.
If I see her in that town,
where the high price of silence is still cheaper than scandal,
if I see her with her in-laws,
black eyeliner and mascara
so heavy on broken-glass eyes with blond hair.

Prodigal

Champs-Elysées

Every day I walk the bridges in the city,
among sand-colored and pink-tinged buildings
past storefronts and sidewalk cafés.
Banks of round marble tables
with gold-back chairs
all facing the same direction.
I see faces: human, animal, mythical,
everywhere you look there's always a face,
and sometimes it is your face.

Along the Champs-Elysées,
the homeless men lie in the middle of the sidewalk.
They are staggered at intervals every block or so.
They lie on their sides or they crouch on their knees.
Each has drawn a chalk balloon above his head.
Inside is written his story.
S'il vous plaît, they all begin,
Then a brief history of their misfortune.
I am without a home in Paris.
I have no job.
I am a poor Frenchman.
I am Jamaican.
They all end, *Merci.*

The men wear suit coats.
They have no belongings,
only a small metal can placed beside them,
empty, or containing a few centimes.
They wear worn leather shoes,
cotton pants with a crease down the front;
and they wear suit jackets,
which they pull over their heads, hiding their faces.

They are impeccable and formal,
bowed down in the middle of the streets,
just the men, lying on their sides,
or in uncomfortable positions.

Chicago

Oh, her money problems were over, that was for sure,
her world got bigger than cellophane noodles with soy sauce
the space around her wood-burning stove,
watching M.A.S.H. every night,
half-hour breaks from studying for her *advanced degree,*
not strong enough *then* to accept money
without feeling beholden.

Oh, she'd been to Chicago, part-time hooker,
worked afternoons at the women's
bakery on Armitage Avenue, whatever.
The air smelled of dead fish blowing up from Lake Michigan.
She'd dropped her camera on her first day there,
watched it bounce down the stone steps
and plunk into the raw water,
tiny waves like dozens of temporary breasts.

When the Firebird scratched out of the drive,
her mother figured she'd never see her daughter again.

Yes, they lived in the Chicano area,
Hell's Angels on the corner
who looked out for them.
Little hippie girls,
eating all that rice and beans.

Evenings, they pulled on hot pants,
see-through tank tops and rode in taxis
paid for by men in glassy
high-rise offices.

What lesbians *do,* they wanted to know.
One guy broke a popper under her nose,
at the right moment
Paid her to seduce the *wife.*

When it was her turn with him,
she ran into the bathroom,
the iridescent tile cold on her foot soles.
"Don't be so sensitive,"
he called after her,
"What are you doing in there?"

Chicago had good radio
bright deejay voices,
good clubs
where girls slow-danced
to Phoebe Snow.
The customers came from the massage parlor
where Dawn worked,
drank coffee from a canteen
strapped to her waist,
ate sesame seeds from
a paper bag with a spoon.
Dawn, with the droopy eyelid,
who otherwise resembled
a miniature Jane Fonda
got herself into tight places, too,
like the time
she got busted for
hand releasing an officer.
Lord.

Dawn called from work every day
asked her what kind of pastry
she wanted her to pick up
on her way home from work.
Oh, she loved pastries.
Not the heavy loaves
from the women's bakery,
but warm *pan dulce*
with pastel stars

of confectioner's sugar,
pink, blue,
pale yellow.
Those were in the days before
anyone knew about hypoglycemic crashes
or keeping ourselves hydrated
and sometimes she was so tired.
She would sit on the steps
of the Mexican bakery,
thinking about home,
where the sky was spanking clean,
the streets a simple silver.

Her mother hadn't said goodbye,
just turned away brittle.
She'd met Dawn in that feminist class
where the guy asked
about lesbians and tweezers.
She explained so gently why
such a question was not worth answering.

That night they'd met at the bar
and she asked,
Can I come back with you
to Chicago? just like that.

At the beginning of her massages,
Dawn always said to the customer,
"It's hot in here. Do you mind if I take off my shirt?"

Days off, they roamed the streets,
down to the filthy beaches.
On these walks,
she realized she'd been searching for this.
wanting to be pushed, pushed too hard,
Pushed on over.

"Alfredo is inviting some friends over,"
Dawn said,
with May wine
to test his waterbed.
"Wanna come?"

Oh yes, she wanted to come.
Oh yes, she'd be into that.

The Fox, 1968

Afternoons, my college roommate in the bottom bunk
draped an arm to shield her eyes.
I studied her in sleep.
At six p.m. she'd rise to meet her fullback boyfriend,
smear foundation makeup on her face
with dutiful indifference
the way I polished saddle oxfords
stripped white liquid down each lace.

She told me stories as I lay above her in the dark,
how Wyandot Indians painted rocks
from the river flowing by her house.
I knew that river, its clay-streaked banks,
gaunt with drought or slick with flood,
but had never known how a beloved
transforms in a lover's gaze:
the burnt cinnamon of her eyes
the color of Big Sandy's mud,
the cast of her pale hands, and now aware,
the texture of her skin and lips and hair.
We would head for North Dakota,
board the Greyhound bus in front of Battson Drugs.
Two thousand miles away might be enough.

She calls me late, whispering, her household asleep.
At three a.m. she remembers best
the time before we knew how thoroughly he'd won.
She calls to tell me Sandy Dennis died,
Banford, from *The Fox,*
killed so many times already,
as we'd watched and watched,
the unfailing crash of that enormous oak,
as we held hands in the movies under her
round-collared coat, that year.

Banford, doomed by her desire,
the only explanation anywhere.

We stopped ourselves from getting on the bus,
but not the kiss that began in winter and did not end till June
the beds stripped down to ticking, neither coming back
her pressing me against the thin door as we stood,
a temporary lock, to finish what we'd both agreed to hide
while his fists pounded, his fullback's body
leaning into me, calling to her, from the other side.

www.ingramcontent.com/pod-product-compliance
Lightning Source LLC
LaVergne TN
LVHW050943080826
845145LV00004B/1386